SELF-PORTRAITS
AS   A
REDDENING SKY

SELF-PORTRAITS AS A REDDENING SKY
© Samuel Gilpin / Cathexis Northwest Press

No part of this book may be reproduced without written permission
of the publisher or author, except in reviews and articles.

First Printing: 2024

ISBN: 978-1-952869-91-4

Cover art by Serhii Tyaglovsky
Designed and edited by C. M. Tollefson

Cathexis Northwest Press
cathexisnorthwestpress.com

SELF-PORTRAITS AS A REDDENING SKY

Poems by
Samuel Gilpin

Cathexis Northwest Press

Table of contents

Therefore,
    if anything exists and is comprehended,
            it is incommunicable.
  –Gorgias

(A LITTLE LIFE)

caught in time as disarray

white hair
melting
in the warm air

there is not enough necessity
in being here alone

truth itself is constructed

the rocks stand
against the wind

1

(AMOR FATI)

light skews across
our faces
stilled

in a sequence

of many indivisible nows

structure
as the means   to reach essence

this notion of inspiration
like the same murky shadow

only the
rain escapes us

(CAREFUL PLANNING)

first shadow
            light gray
in the rainy morning

                                    the desire for writing
                              to be the end of its
                              own activity

there are no properties which are absolute
                        which are essential

                              a pale blue
                                    delivery truck
                                    turning down the narrow street

                        in the world everything is as it is

(CAN LIFE GET ANY BETTER)

far pines
stiff in wind

this silence tightly woven

prairie sloping
to river plane

silent bird of prey

high above

you say try to love
the scattered bits
and pieces

of this larger vision

when i die
i hope
i'm remembered

(CROSSING THE BROWN LAND)

cracked
horizon
undone

frozen river

unbroken

the key to your house in my pocket

i remember thinking i know not what to do

your body rooted in silence

(CRIMSON BETWEEN BLACK AND ROSE)

dust in air
seeping into topsoil

a blue afternoon

nature is that which is kept forbidden

the burnt landscape

still nothing else

we've been
finding
word's hollowness

my god i need you

(CRYSTALLINE)

dark streak of land
    flanked by swell

tugboat anchored

    in fog

    and the grey tree weeps

        we use music to explain
          the experience of time

we are
    urged to seek
    the highest good

(EVERY MAN FOR HIMSELF)

there are
languages here
and yet i understand
none of them

observational

frames of reference
moving inward

a scratch across
the still landscape
and all is hidden

(GHOST IN THE MACHINE)

a glass of wine
on the table

the soft cleft
of the apricot

the referential
fetish in language

i pull the covers over my head
thinking things used to feel
so pretty
so innocent

in order to remain
silent

you must have something to say

(I'VE SAID MY PIECE)

grove of cottonwoods
debris of rock and twig

this earnest attempt
to set in order
the facts of experience

this strong desire to be strong

a sun born
to abstraction
concealed by
shade of trees

the telling of a dream
is quite a different matter

than dreaming itself

(IRIDESCENCE)

brown weed
off bank

torn green paper
carried by wind

the gray sky's creamy

responding to such tenderness
i'm afraid you'll
leave me all alone

holding a color
photo of a young girl

thinking things used to feel so pretty

low hung kitchen light
oblique and quiet

(LANDSCAPE OF NEW SNOW)

the window
reflects

                    and the curtain
                      fills the background

      tonight
        you said
        i am too tired

           replace the performance of language by presence

     closeness
     and distance
     are relative conditions

(LET THE WIND SPEAK)

pale sand

shale light
under running water

from where do feelings arise

river bank
withdrawn from sky

(ORIGINS OF REPLICATION)

pale figure of speech

partially drawn curtains

one pink blossom

tucked behind your ear

light slanting
through the kitchen window

i know that i am not here

they say there is no hope

(THIN FILIGREE)

dawn light

gray
above the river

the far pines

stiff
in wind

beauty spooling
inside me

i've woke alone to the myth of my life

(UTOPIA)

                      flash of light
            along suburban
                  horizon

                              you sit smoking
                                ash growing longer

one worry breaking off

        as another
      takes hold

                              there's something really very nice
                                  about a voice that isn't articulating into words

                              i'll come back
                              each night
                                      with a different name

(VOICE CRYING IN THE WILDERNESS)

dead afternoon
drifting in

blue as memory's air

this is how

beauty

works

a blanket laid upon the grass

a ripe persimmon

on the countertop

Samuel Gilpin is a poet living in Portland, OR,
who holds a Ph.D. in English Lit. from the University of Nevada, Las Vegas,
which explains why he works as a door to door salesman. A Prism Review Poetry Contest winner,
he has served as the Poetry Editor of Witness Magazine and Book Review Editor of Interim.
A Cleveland State University First Book Award finalist, his work has appeared in various journals
and magazines, most recently in The Bombay Gin, Omniverse, and Colorado Review.

Also Available
from
Cathexis Northwest Press:

Cathexis Northwest Press

Printed in the USA
CPSIA information can be obtained
at www.ICGtesting.com
CBHW081706240924
14863CB00060B/1435